SIMPLY SCIENCE

Sinking and Floating

by Natalie M. Rosinsky

Content Adviser: Mats Selen, Ph.D.,
Department of Physics, University of Illinois at Champaign-Urbana

Science Adviser: Terrence E. Young Jr., M.Ed., M.L.S.,
Jefferson Parish (La.) Public Schools

Reading Adviser: Dr. Linda D. Labbo,
Department of Reading Education, College of Education,
The University of Georgia

COMPASS POINT BOOKS
MINNEAPOLIS, MINNESOTA

Compass Point Books
3109 West 50th Street, #115
Minneapolis, MN 55410

Visit Compass Point Books on the Internet at *www.compasspointbooks.com*
or e-mail your request to *custserv@compasspointbooks.com*

Photographs ©: PhotoDisc, cover, 4, 5, 11, 12, 16; Image Select/Art Resource, N.Y., 6; Index Stock
Imagery, 7; Gregg Andersen, 8; BrandXPictures, 10; Jennie Woodcock/Reflections Photolibrary/
Corbis, 15; Hulton/Archive by Getty Images, 17; Library of Congress, 19; Stockbyte, 20; Corbis, 21;
Jeffrey L. Rotman/Corbis, 23; Defense Visual Information Center, 24; John Mielcarek/Dembinsky
Photo Associates, 27; Wolfgang Kaehler/Corbis, 28; Creatas, 29; John Cross/The Free Press, 32.

Editor: Catherine Neitge
Photo Researcher: Svetlana Zhurkina
Designer/Page Production: Bradfordesign, Inc./The Design Lab

Library of Congress Cataloging-in-Publication Data
Rosinsky, Natalie M. (Natalie Myra)
    Sinking and floating / by Natalie Rosinsky.
        p. cm. — (Simply science)
Summary: A brief introduction to how and why different objects sink or float.
Includes bibliographical references and index.
    ISBN 0-7565-0598-4 (hardcover)
1. Floating bodies—Juvenile literature. [1. Floating bodies.] I. Title. II. Series: Simply science
(Minneapolis, Minn.)
    QC147.5.R67 2004
    532'.25—dc22   2003014415

Table of Contents

*Note: In this book, words that are defined in the glossary are in **bold** the first time they appear in the text.*

Watch and Wonder

Watch a leaf. It floats across a pond. See a boat. Even filled with people, it floats on lakes and oceans. Did you ever wonder why? Drop a small stone into water. Watch it quickly sink. Your wonder will grow! Yet sinking and floating are not really mysteries. Let's learn about the different reasons they happen.

◀ Boats filled with people float on the water.

Maple leaves float on the water. ▶

On Top or Below?

Long ago, the Greek scientist Archimedes sat in a bathtub. He figured out some important ideas by seeing the water he had **displaced!** You can learn by doing, too.

Gather some small things together. They can be natural or manufactured.

You might try a pinecone, a piece of **cork,** and a lemon. You could test a safety pin, a marble, and a penny. Hold each one in your hand. Which things feel light? Which are heavier? Now, put each one into a large bowl filled with water. Which things float on top? Which things sink below?

Many things float when you put them in water. Their weight does not pull them all the way under the surface. This is

Archimedes experimented with water in his bathtub.

A pinecone floats.

because water pushes up on any
object that you put into it. This
upward force is called **buoyancy**.
It depends on how much liquid

the object has pushed out of the way. The pinecone and the cork float. Their weight is not big enough to overcome the buoyant force. The marble and the penny sink. Their weight is bigger than the buoyant force.

But what about the lemon and the safety pin? The sunny fruit is heavier than the marble and penny. Yet it floats! The steel safety pin weighs less than the marble, penny, or the lemon. Yet the safety pin sinks! Are you surprised? There is more to sinking and floating than weight alone.

Some things float and some do not. A pinecone, lemon, and cork float. A marble, penny, and safety pin do not.

More than Heavy

Some things are heavy for their size. Take a piece of steel. Now take a piece of cork or plastic that is the same size. The steel weighs more. We say that the **density** of steel is greater than the density of cork or plastic. Steel is a **dense** material. Dense materials usually sink. So, now you know that when you put an object in a liquid, the

An orange slice will rise to the top and float.

Plastic fishing bobbers float on the water.

liquid will push up on it. The size of this push is equal to the weight of the liquid that has been pushed out of the way by the object. Here is the scientific way to say this: The buoyant force is equal to the weight of the displaced liquid. This rule makes it easy for scientists to figure out if something will sink or float.

If an object is more dense than a liquid, it will sink when you put it in the liquid. If an object

A safety pin is made of dense steel.

is less dense than a liquid, it will float when you put it in the liquid. A piece of steel is more dense than water, so it sinks in water. A piece of cork or plastic is less dense than water, so it floats in water. This is true for big things and little things. Even though it is very small and light, a safety pin sinks. That is because it is made of dense steel. The safety pin's small size does not displace enough water to make it float.

The shape of objects also affects sinking and floating. You *can* make a heavy or dense thing float! Take a ball of clay. Put it into a bowl of water. Watch how quickly it sinks. The upward push of water is no match for the downward push of this object. Now, reshape the clay into a wide boat. Will your boat float inside the bowl? Yes, indeed!

By stretching out the clay into the shape of a boat, you increase its surface. You have increased the amount of water the clay is able to push out of the way. As long as the clay boat can displace its own weight in water, it will float. We say that the clay boat is buoyant.

A ball of clay will sink, but clay made into a wide boat will float. ▶

Because Air Is There

In the 1840s, people did not believe that a steel ship would float. An engineer named Isambard Kingdom Brunel showed it could be done.

Steel ships are built with extra spaces just for air. These spaces called bulkheads help the ships float. Air weighs much less than steel. Air even weighs less than water. All of these spaces

Ships have bulkheads to help them float.

Isambard Kingdom Brunel designed ships in the mid-1800s.

filled with air make it possible for a ship to displace a lot of water. Therefore, the ship can float!

In 1912, the largest passenger ship ever built was put to sea. The *Titanic* had 15 bulkheads. It was supposed to be unsinkable. Yet the *Titanic* sank on its very first trip after it hit a large iceberg. Too many of its bulkheads were destroyed. All of the air spaces filled up with water. Since the *Titanic* could not displace enough water, it sank.

You can see how air helps something float. Take an empty glass jar. Screw the lid on tight. It is empty

The Titanic sank in April 1912 after ▶
hitting an iceberg.

of everything but air! Put the jar
in a bowl filled with water. Watch
it float. Also notice the level of the
water in the bowl. See how much

it rises when you put in the jar. This is because the jar displaces some water when it floats.

A lemon floats because its skin has pockets of air. Ducks and geese float for a similar reason. Their feathers contain tiny tubes filled with air. Sometimes, young swimmers use air-filled water wings to stay afloat!

The feathers on geese have tiny tubes filled with air.

Water wings keep a girl afloat.

Getting Shipshape

Ships that float may also sink. There have been many shipwrecks. Sometimes, ships carrying **cargo** sink. Their loads were too heavy or uneven. You can see this happen with your clay boat. Put some pennies in the center of the boat. See it float lower as the load increases. How many pennies will finally sink your boat? Start again. This time, place pennies only on one side. How quickly does the boat sink now? Today, there are laws limiting the amount of cargo ships can carry.

Fish swim around the wreck of a ship that sank near Grand Cayman in the Caribbean.

Sailors have learned to arrange loads evenly.

Some boats are supposed to sink. They usually travel underwater. These **submarines** have special tanks called ballasts. When the captain gives the order, water is let into the ballast tanks. The extra weight of this water helps the submarine sink. When it is time to surface, **pumps** push the water out of the ballast tanks. They add air instead. This air helps the submarine reach the surface and float.

◀ *The USS* Maine *is one of the U.S. Navy's newest submarines.*

Like Oil and Water

Some liquids are denser than others. Water is denser than oil. You can test this yourself. Pour some vegetable oil into a glass. Then add some water. Stir and wait. The liquids will separate. In a while, the yellow oil will float on top of the water. The clear, denser water has sunk below. Sometimes when people argue, we say they get along "like oil and water." This means that they do not mix well together!

The shiny, rainbow colors in street puddles come from oil. Some

Oil floats on top of water. ▶

cars and trucks drip oil. This oil rises
to the top of the water puddles.

Some water is actually denser
than other water! Salt increases the

density of water. This is why people float so well in the extra-salty Dead Sea. This very salty lake is between Israel and Jordan. Its water pushes up with more force than regular ocean water.

Do you swim or sail? Perhaps you play in the tub! You may wash dishes at home. All these activities are more fun when you know about sinking and floating.

A woman reads a magazine while floating in the Dead Sea.

Floating in the swimming pool is extra fun when you know all about it.

Glossary

buoyancy—the upward force on something caused by the liquid it is in

cargo—the goods carried in a ship

cork—a lightweight kind of wood, sometimes used to keep bottles closed

dense—something that is heavy for its size

density—how heavy something is for its size

displaced—moved away from its original place or position

pumps—machines that move liquid or gas from one place to another

submarines—ships that usually travel underwater

Did You Know?

- Big, heavy logs float because they are not as dense as water.

- Water gets bigger when it freezes. Icebergs float because they are less dense than water.

Want to Know More?

At the Library

Cole, Joanna. *The Magic School Bus Ups and Downs: A Book About Floating and Sinking.*
  New York: Scholastic, 1997.

Gordon, Maria. *Float and Sink.* New York: Thomson Learning, 1995.

Humble, Richard. *Submarines and Ships.* New York: Viking, 1998.

Rowe, Julian, and Molly Perham. *Keep It Afloat!* Chicago: Childrens Press, 1993.

On the Web

For more information on *sinking and floating,* use
FactHound to track down Web sites related to this book.

1. Go to *www.compasspointbooks.com/facthound*
2. Type in this book ID: 0756505984
3. Click on the *Fetch It* button.

Your trusty FactHound will fetch the best Web sites for you!

Through the Mail

The Mariners' Museum

100 Museum Drive

Newport News, VA 23606

For information about exhibits and classes for kids on maritime science and history

On the Road

The Submarine Force Museum

Groton, CT

800/343-0071

To visit a Navy museum about submarines used since the Revolutionary War and
take a tour inside the USS *Nautilus*

Index

About the Author

Natalie M. Rosinsky writes about science, economics, history, and other fun things. One of her two cats usually sits on her computer as she works in Mankato, Minnesota. Natalie earned graduate degrees from the University of Wisconsin and has been a high school and college teacher.